WHAT IS MY BEDROOM MADE OF?

Written by
ALEX HALL

MATERIALS AT HOME

Library of Congress Control Number:
The Library of Congress Control Number is available on the Library of Congress website.

ISBN
979-8-89359-429-4 (library bound)
979-8-89359-449-2 (paperback)
979-8-89359-487-4 (epub)
979-8-89359-469-0 (hosted ebook)

Printed in the United States of America
Mankato, MN
012026

sales@northstareditions.com
888-417-0195

Written by:
Alex Hall

Edited by:
Noah Leatherland

Designed by:
Amy Li

PHOTO CREDITS

ALL IMAGES ARE COURTESY OF SHUTTERSTOCK.COM, UNLESS OTHERWISE STATED.
Recurring – fire_fly, xnova. Cover – Alhovik, JOJOSTUDIO, mStudioVector, picoStudio, The Studio, Inside Creative House, Jamroen_Photo Background, New Africa, Anton Starikov. 4–5 – FamVeld, Joaquin Corbalan P. 6–7 – domnitsky, Ground Picture, mustafaozelsancak, Pixel-Shot. 8–9 – New Africa, Regreto, Yuganov Konstantin. 10–11 – sasimoto, SeventyFour, Yuri-U. 12–13 – Foxtories, New Africa, OlhaTsiplya. 14–15 – K'Nub, PeopleImages.com – Yuri A. Tomsickova Tatyana. 16–17 – New Africa, PeopleImages.com – Yuri A. 18–19 – Andrei Zveaghintev, nexus 7, noprati somchit. 20–21 – Alex Staroseltsev, Dima Moroz, Irina Gutyryak, New Africa, Photobac. 22–23 – Ground Picture, Sorapop Udomsri.

CONTENTS

Words that look like **this** can be found in the glossary on page 24.

WHAT ARE MATERIALS?

There are many things that you can see and touch in your bedroom. These things are called objects. Objects are made of materials. Materials can be natural or human-made.

All materials have properties. Properties are ways of describing what something is like. Materials can be soft, hard, sturdy, or bendy. There are many different properties that materials can have.

MY BED

My bed frame is made of wood. Wood is a natural material. It comes from trees. Most wood is strong and durable. Its strength makes it a great material to use for a bed frame.

Most beds are made of wood or metal. What is your bed made of?

The bed also needs a comfy mattress. Part of my mattress is made of foam. Foam is a soft and flexible material. It bends to support my body as I sleep.

MY PILLOWS

COTTON

My pillows are made of cotton. Cotton is a natural material that comes from a plant. It is very soft. My pillowcase is made of a thin cotton fabric.

Inside my pillow, there is a soft cotton stuffing. Big, fluffy pillows support my neck and head. These pillows help me get a good night's sleep.

What color is your pillowcase?

MY CHAIR

My chair's legs are made of a metal called steel. Steel is a human-made material. It's strong enough to hold someone's weight when they sit down.

FACT: Steel is easy to clean.

The covering of my chair is made of a material called nylon. Nylon is used because it is comfortable to sit on. It is also strong and tough to break.

MY DRESSER

My dresser is made of wood, just like my bed. Wood is used for many objects because it is so strong. Wood can also easily be cut into different shapes.

The clothes in my dresser are made of many different materials. My sweater is made of wool. Wool is good at trapping heat. It will keep me warm in cold weather.

WOOL

Do you have any wool clothes in your dresser?

MY TOYS

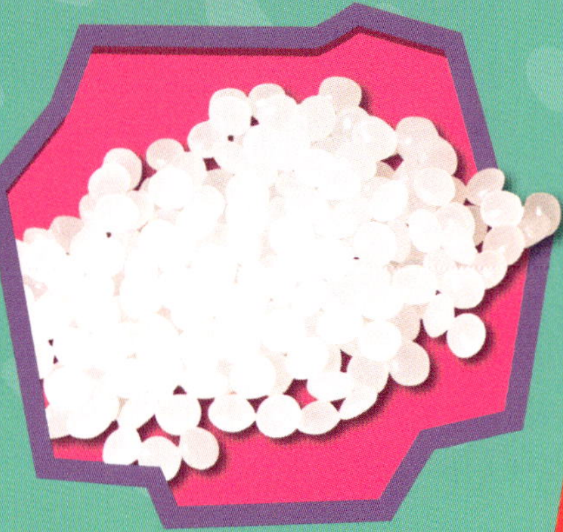

PLASTIC

Lots of my toys are made of plastic. Plastic is human-made. It can be made into many different shapes and colors. This is why so many toys are made using plastic.

Plastic is a strong and durable material. It can last for hundreds of years. Try to donate old toys instead of throwing them away. This is better for the planet.

FACT:
You can give your old toys to charity.

MY BOOKS

PAPER

My books are made of paper. Paper comes from trees. Paper is a light and flexible material. It can bend easily without breaking.

What is your favorite book?

FACT:
People have used paper to make books for hundreds of years.

Paper is a very useful material. It can be cut into different shapes and sizes. People can print and write on paper. Paper is a great material to use for books.

MY WINDOW

My window is made of glass. Glass is a human-made material. It is transparent. You can see through it. People use glass to make windows because it lets sunlight into a room.

Glass windows are strong. They are difficult to shatter. Glass windows can withstand lots of rain and wind without breaking.

What can you see outside your bedroom window?

SPOT THE

MATERIALS

Which of these objects is made of wood?

NIGHTSTAND

CURTAINS

TEDDY BEAR

Only the nightstand is made of wood. The teddy bear and the curtains are made of cotton.

Which of these objects is made of glass?

LIGHT BULB

DESK

RUG

Only the light bulb is made of glass. The desk is made of wood, and the rug is made of wool.

WHAT IS IN YOUR BEDROOM?

There are so many materials that make up our bedrooms. Materials are chosen based on their properties. Choosing the right material means the object can do its job properly.

Your bedroom might have objects that are made of many different materials. Look at something in your bedroom. Do you know what that object is made of? Why was that material used?

GLOSSARY

DESCRIBING	saying what something is like
DONATE	to give something away for a cause such as charity
DURABLE	not easily broken or worn out
FABRIC	material made by weaving threads of cotton, wool, nylon, silk, or other fibers
NATURAL	found in nature and not made by people

INDEX